Modern Child's Prayer

Martha Tess Little

Modern Child's Prayer © 2023 Martha Tess Little

All rights reserved.

No part of this publication may be reproduced, stored in a retrieval system, or transmitted, in any form or by any means, electronic, mechanical, photocopying, recording or otherwise, without the prior written permission of the presenters.

Martha Tess Little asserts the moral right to be identified as author of this work.

Presentation by *BookLeaf Publishing*

Web: www.bookleafpub.com

E-mail: info@bookleafpub.com

ISBN: 9789357696968

First edition 2023

DEDICATION

To Brooke, Brandy, Josie, Avery, Catherine, Ryan, Meg, Kenlee

They heard it all first and dealt with me at my worst.

My Toys

Our youth is stripped away
like the toys out of our hands

One tells us to sit
The other says to stand

They call us kids
but expect us to act as adults

Then we make one mistake
and they say "It's all your fault"

I'm sorry that I'm a child
I'm sorry that I'm not allowed to have fun
I'm sorry that all I do is sit
cause I was told I could not run

Now they all are saying
"Enjoy your youth while you can"

How may I
when you took it away

like the toy I would once hold when I pray

But I don't pray much anymore

Bet you wonder why
Bet you think I'm corrupt
and all that all my doings are just sly

Really you all just hurt me
No, not my God up above
It was those who stripped me of my toys
and my smiles
and my cheers

It is those who you can thank for all my sadness
All my screams
All my tears

My Old Song

I once wrote a song
It was about a road
and a bike
and my friends along the way

It pictured us riding into the sunset
Pure joy is all we felt
In flowing white dresses
Our innocence on the shelf

The scene had been so familiar to me
I experienced it every other week
Years later now
Its all I seek

In a Corner

In a corner you can see
Although it is enclosing
I find it free
The room is exposed to my eye
I can see it all
They don't notice when I cry
Looking out on the room
I try to consume
To look is to learn
And to learn is to grow
As I find myself getting bigger
I wonder a lot
Why everyone always fought
Over land
Over people
Over love and beautiful things
If they just looked from my corner
Truth they would see
My corner is perfect
I don't ever want to leave

Future's Gleam

I hope that once I'm out there
it is how I want it to be
I'll get to do, see, and become me
My books will be best sellers
My thoughts will be shared with the world
I'll live up to my big name
My big Little name

College will be fun
I won't drink too much
But I'll get to dance
I'll turn down boys
who think they have a chance
My brother will show me all the best places
and teach me all the songs
I'll be his designated driver
Stop him from doing too many wrongs

My speech will be short
and sweet as cold pop
The lights won't blind me
all the way at the top
I'll grab my award

Golden in sheen
"I've waited for this day my whole life"
My smile will beam

The group chat will all move away
Don't worry we stay in touch
Kenlee's in Cali
Josie in Oregon
Avery on Massachusetts Bay
Every year we get together
in a summer home
Two of our kids fall in love
a Jenny Han type tome

I am happy, free,
unapologetically me,
craving the next adventure
while having a spot of tea
My life is ahead
It won't stop there
I need to take a break
Breathe in the now air

Raised To

I was raised to be a ceo's wife
Told how to dress to attract a man
Told when you smile
And shake a hand
Told which opinions to take a stand
And the ones to keep deep down

I was raised to be strong
But get yelled at when I cry
So obviously I cry more
Then go and lie
Saying I'm sore
Actually my body's about to die

The image of me is in a golden frame
It's one I do not claim
That picture is doctored to be another person
One who effortlessly gets the grade
One who smiles a braceless smile
One who sings the Beatles in the clouds

That golden frame has a reverse

Its black felt flush against the wall
It leaves an imprint of me I recognize when
night calls
One of studying tear marked papers
One of forcing a retainer into my mouth
One of singing rigid Pink Floyd
"Welcome to the Machine"

I was raised to live this life
Honestly I live it quite well
I do what needs to be done
So what it's not always fun
What Momma said has helped me fight
I am now hard to fright
I am thankful in the end
I get to honor my family name
One day I'll be our claim to fame

Your Power

Most people don't know the power they have
to speak and not be mocked
Some of us are stopped by repeating voices
that leave us totally blocked
skipping over the important parts
The parts we want to share

We have to get others to read our words aloud,
ones with the power,
Please don't mistake my words for their own
thoughts
They came from my own traumatized brain
typed by these calloused fingers

Your power is something I would die for
Something I have dumped money into since I
was 6
Gone to countless doctors who still can't find a
fix

PLease, I am begging, don't waste your power

Use it for ones taken out of class
Use it for ones who have to live in their heads
Use it for the little ones who can't say "here"
cause the teacher won't let them get it out
Use it for ones who can't get a job cause they
can't say their name
Use it for the ones who when given the option to
speak or to fly would have to think
Use your power for me
So that they can all one day see

Dancing Papers

I lost a slip of paper
On it my heart and soul
My insides are beating
Ripping out of my chest
I must find that paper
Till I do I won't rest

Everything is on that paper
Addressed to the unexpecting
Lines of the truth
Spit out like shotgun shells
Crumbled up
Straightened all stout
Almost burnt to a crisp till I pussied out

Head racing
Paper running
Always just beyond my horizon
I need it back
What it holds is dangerous

This paper is a knife

Written to be sharp
I spent days on it
Looked over it carefully like art
It's not beautiful like a painting, though,
Unless tragedy is to be adored

Days
And the paper is still away
I can't find even a fray
I know someone has saw
Embarrassed to call
They can't know I'm looking

My paper will dance
Beyond the grasp of hand
Till the wind pushes it back
While I wait I will rewrite
This time holding it tight

Tranparent

Being made of glass doesn't seem to be enough,
Though how immensely transparent one is.
What people don't seem to get is that the clarity
allows them to see everything
The bad…
The good…
The evil…
Any person with good intentions will lead those
they care for to a place that when they look
through there is beauty
Too bad good intentions rarely travel through the
selfish solidity of the common man

The Weeds

Notice the one who hasn't been exposed
he thinks the weeds are pretty
but when the wind blows
She spreads her disease all below the trees
She takes from the twigs the grass and the leaves

She's killing them all
Those directed and not
She kills them all
Without even a thought
His garden is ruined
His estate of love
It's all gone
Not leaving a bug

Planting has stopped
And the seasons are long
Everyone left
Singing went along
He didn't see the pain
It blew a mile astray
The sneezes all warned
But he wouldn't stay away

She's killing him all
The weeds
The weeds

Following the Rain

I never believed in a rainbow after the rain…
They would always just appear.
I never believed a rainbow to be full either… It
was always just the primary colors
I believed this all till one fine day at twilight,
when I caught myself distracted by the sky, as I
always did.
It had just rained.
My shoes were full of water.
The clouds had all cleared out.
There was just the faint shimmer of appearing
stars against a periwinkle sky that drifted from
blue to purple…
And there it was.
ALL its colors enhanced by the mise en scene…
My only rainbow after the rain.

Red Lobby Bench

They took our bench away
We couldn't even say goodbye
We all thought we had more time
guess that was a lie
I can't believe it's totally gone
with no group picture we can look upon
Its red painted seems
will never seat anymore pants
we will never throw our backpacks down to
dance,
and after a long learning day,
when we just need a place to go to bed
That red lobby bench
will be pictured in our heads

Loud Classrooms

Quiet classes are where we reside
Packed like sardines
Shoulders side to side
The boys all muscly and broad
The girls sharp and boney
Others lost in between

Loud classrooms are what I miss
With polka dot walls
Speaking in secret calls
We're all side by side
None left out or off guard
A kind hearted psyche
Leading little wandering souls
Outfitted all in pudgy shells

Academic Validation Nation

All the signs say "TURN AROUND"
Still I stride forward
I pass the things they warned me of
Like the walking dead
Elongated sheets marked up in red
Stapled to their heads
Their test scores carved into their arms
The papers cover their eyes
Not only dead
But blind
Still they move like their alive

The farther I go
The darker it gets
The more concentrated too
Heads are off in books
Students jailed by backpack hooks
Essays upon essays suffocating them all
Leads to another hall

Walls are chalkboards
Covered in endless math
It's a never ending

Continuing path
The dead have pulled their papers up
To look at their life's work
They stand back and gock
Their miniscule errors
Kill them with shock

The hall opens up
After miles of lives
A sea gapes down
In I dive
Trying to escape the frowns
The waters glassy
In it reflects me
I have red on my face
And numbers on my arms
I should have listened to the signs
I have now lost my mind

Someone Fix

Break out
Break free
Break in
Break me
Break you
Break her
Break him
Break them

We all break

Break hearts
Break souls
Break bones
Break toys
Break girls
Break boys
Break glass
Break stone

We all break

So why will no one fix

John Lennon and I

John Lennon said he was a "nowhere man"
What if that's what I really am?
Relentlessly chasing this dream to be
always too blinded to see
John Lennon made himself great
and I took the bait
thought that could be me too
I didn't see the laughter cue

Walk Our Mile

Walk our mile
Follow the line
Keep up the pace
We're running out of time

Leave your head hung down
Move as one in the vast sea
Don't stand out
It's a sure way to drown

Walk our mile
On a made up path
Our leader guides us
While we're filled with wrath

Box TVs

Box TVs sum up life
A Heavy weight
yet holds a canvas of imagination `
They can take you on soaring flights
or to the trench fights
All through a little disc
we have now stored out of sight